In the Shadow of a Maverick Copy

Lessons from my father

Erika Nomland Cilengir

Rainmaker Publishing

First edition

Paperback ISBN: 978-1-961351-00-4

In memory of my parents, whose unconditional love, devotion to their values, and joie de vivre have given me strength, optimism, and joy.

"I am because other people are." ~ Desmond Tutu

Contents

1. Introduction   1

   That smile

   A family legacy of risk-taking and courage

   Early influences

   Hand in glove

   Mining our parents' legacies for life lessons

   A nod to historical and personal veracity

2. Lesson 1 – Art is Essential   13

   An artist at heart

   Jazz, blues, and rock n' roll

   The Fine Arts Group

   Every ruin has a story

   A marriage of site and structure

   Christmas cards as works of art with a message

   How this lesson guided my life

3. Lesson 2 – Discovery Without Play is Not Possible   25

   Playing in the dirt

   Imaginary worlds under the covers

A community lot

Evening board games

Quiet time

The studio

How this lesson guided my life

4. Lesson 3 – Your Values Have No Offramps   35

Risking disdain

Risking arrest

Risking rejection

Encouraging resistance

Encouraging creation

Encouraging belonging

How this lesson guided my life

5. Lesson 4 – Peace is Always an Option   43

War is not an option

A life taken does not justify a life taken

Guns have no place in our world

Alternatives to war

Respect for the peacemakers

Civil disobedience

How this lesson guided my life

6. Lesson 5 – Justice is All or Nothing   51

Harnessing the democratic process

Banishing otherness

Travel as a gateway to understanding

Protest as patriotism

Living with diversity

Respect for all creatures

How this lesson guided my life

7. Reflecting on the Lessons I've Learned   63

    Honoring the lesson givers

    Owning our lessons

    Casting away the shadow

    Final thoughts

Acknowledgments   69

About the Author   71

Chapter One

Introduction

"May we all find a little of the enchantment our world has to offer."
~ Kemper Nomland, Jr.

S hortly after my Dad, Kemper Nomland, Jr., passed away on Christmas Day 2009, a friend sent me a message that included the following: "In the Jewish tradition, only very good people die on special holidays." It proved to be one of the most comforting messages I received in the wake of Dad's death. I already knew what a loving and supportive father he had always been, but I have only fully appreciated what a remarkable life he led in the intervening years since his death.

Dad's humility was one of his hallmark traits. He was the antithesis of a self-promoter. He rarely spoke of the past, although he would have had many engaging and inspiring stories to tell. And he never touted his accomplishments, although he had many to tout. He touched countless people in innumerable positive ways.

Dad could easily have been Ralph Waldo Emerson's muse in his "What is Success" poem, one of my favorites:

"To laugh often and much;

To win the respect of intelligent people and

the affection of children;

To earn the approbation of honest critics and endure

the betrayal of false friends;

To appreciate beauty;

To find the best in others;

To give of one's self;

To leave the world a bit better, whether by a healthy child,

a garden patch, or a redeemed social condition;

To have played and laughed with enthusiasm and

sung with exultation;

To know even one life has breathed easier because you

have lived—

This is to have succeeded."

Dad was indeed a "very good person." To understand the foundation that molded him into what he was to become, it is helpful to know a bit about his character, his roots, his early influences, and his choice in a life partner.

That smile

Dad's smile was everything. It was genuine and disarming and reflected the joy he found in all corners of his life. He was the quintessential optimist. There was no problem too big to be solved and, god knows, he took on some of the biggest in his lifetime—to abolish war and vanquish injustice.

Folks meeting him for the first time were often already familiar with some aspect of his legacy and were quick to acknowledge it. He didn't let a compliment linger for long. His radiant smile and a short thank you were all that he indulged. Then it was on to other topics.

The only times a smile did not grace his face were when the world was crossing him—in its impulse to wage war, in the wake of a mass shooting, or in its hate and scapegoating. I only remember one time when he did not greet me with a smile and it was justified. I was perhaps 10 years old and whining unrelentingly about not getting what I wanted. That experience was memorable because it was so rare and it pained me to realize I had been the initiator of such a rare event. I was ashamed that I had destroyed, if only briefly, the thing I cherished most about Dad—his smile—and the comfort and hope it gave me.

A family legacy of risk-taking and courage

That Dad had the strength of character to take on issues most shied away from is easy to understand when you examine his family history. Like many Americans, Dad was the descendent of immigrant grandparents on both his mother's and father's sides.

*Fred & Alice Barrington
& Family.*

His maternal grandparents were Canadians by birth with ancestral roots in the British Isles and Holland. His maternal grandfather, Fred Barrington, was a railroad man, drawn to the United States by the promise of cheap land available under the Homestead Act of 1862, which provided 160 acres to any adult citizen or intended citizen if they agreed to "improve" their plot. His wife, Dad's maternal grandmother, Alice Ransier Barrington, accompanied her husband into the wilderness of what would become North Dakota, but not without enforcing some of her own demands. After having to give birth to their first child with no support—medical or familial—and losing the child, Alice made it clear that the next time she was pregnant, she would return to her family and medical network in her hometown of Athens in Ontario, Canada. And that is exactly what she did when my Great Aunt Ethel was born. Ultimately, Fred and Alice Barrington successfully homesteaded land in both North Dakota and Montana, relying on themselves and a scattering of other pioneers to withstand the inhospitable winters and harsh conditions of life without conveniences. Later in life, Alice was also an active Prohibitionist with a lifetime membership in the Women's Christian Temperance Union. Ironically, at the end of her life, Alice enjoyed a glass of sherry at bedtime.

Knut and Sarah Nomland.

Whereas Dad's paternal grandmother, Sarah, was a second-generation immigrant, his paternal grandfather was a first-generation immigrant, both born of Norwegian parents. Knut Nomland, his paternal grandfather, immigrated as a child to the land that would later be christened North Dakota. As an adult, Knut was drawn to public service, and served as the second State Treasurer of North Dakota and the only Democratic-Independent State Treasurer among the first 25 State Treasurers. Knut and Sarah Nomland were also founding members of the Grue Lutheran Church in Traill County, North Dakota.

Although Dad did not have close relationships with his grandparents because of time and distance, they endowed him with an innate strength and determination to tackle challenges, stand up for his values, and give back.

Early influences

Unlike his parents, Dad was born in Los Angeles, where he resided for his entire life. While he initially lived in the City of Los Angeles, Dad later moved with his family to Altadena. Dad's childhood growing up in the greater Los Angeles area was a far cry from the childhoods of his parents, Elgie and Kemper Nomland, Sr. As a former schoolteacher and graduate of Columbia University, with a degree in Architecture, respectively, Dad's mother and father were strong advocates for education.

Kemper and Elgie Nomland,
Sr. and sons, John & Kemper.

Dad was a product of the public school system from elementary through junior college. Among the public schools Dad attended was Washington Junior High School in Pasadena, California. There he shared classes with a handful of Blacks, Asians, and Latinos, including future Hall of Famer and social justice advocate,

Jackie Robinson, who signed Dad's class picture, "Jack Robinson "35"," referring to the Class of 1935. The opportunity to develop friendships with students whose backgrounds differed from his own likely had a positive impact on Dad at an impressionable age.

Architecture also played an oversized role in Dad's early life. Kemper Nomland, Sr. was a member of the team of architects tasked with designing a new Los Angeles City Hall, one of Los Angeles' most recognizable public buildings. It is unclear how prominently art figured in the lives of Dad's parents, but they nurtured Dad's artistic leanings early on. Just out of high school, Dad aspired to make a living as an artist and accepted an internship with Diego Rivera. However, even back then, he admitted that architecture would be his backup career. Indeed, architecture turned out to be more than a "backup career." Dad went on to attend the University of Southern California's School of Architecture and ultimately became better known for his architecture than his art.

Having grown up with my paternal grandparents, I frankly cannot tell you what magic parenting formula they might have used to raise two remarkable sons, the second being my Uncle John. What I can tell you is how I experienced my grandparents. They loved to travel, especially my grandfather, who published journals for family and friends after each trip, including trips to Norway, Cuba, and Mexico (many times). They both worked hard, loved to play bridge, took pride in their home, and emphasized the importance of responsibility. I like to think that their love, support, and guidance resulted in two exemplary sons, who mixed that with their unique understanding of the zeitgeist they lived through and how best to respond to its challenges.

Hand in glove—father's partner in life

Mom & Dad.

My Mom, Ella Kube Nomland, was a tailor-made match for Dad. They met in Los Angeles after the war when Mom was a graduate student at UCLA, completing her doctorate in Psychology. Despite Mom being five years older than Dad, a German immigrant with a wildly different background, Dad found in her a strong, intelligent woman, as equally committed to her values as he was to his. Like Dad, she was a pacifist and a social justice advocate. They both believed in speaking out in defense of one's values.

Mom left Germany in 1933, just as Hitler was establishing a stranglehold on German society. She saw the writing on the wall and did not like the message. After time spent in Great Britain and India, Mom secured a scholarship to attend the College of Emporia in Kansas, where she completed her undergraduate studies, and from there moved to Los Angeles to pursue her doctorate on a full scholarship. In her early 50s, Mom decided to become a U.S. citizen. However, being both a pacifist and an atheist, Mom refused to take the citizenship oath because she refused to bear arms in defense of the United States. Additionally, her pacifism was not derived from religious training or belief in a supreme being. A ground-breaking court case found that Mom's "belief in an ordered universe, one that was not created by any human beings or animals, qualifies as religion."

Mom and Dad were each other's biggest champions. They cheered each other on through all their challenges, including the cancer that killed Mom at the age of 80.

Mining our parents' legacies for life lessons

Have you ever wondered why you are the way you are? Why are you passionate about some things and completely dismissive of other things? These are questions I have been asking myself more and more as I age. Quite naturally, I have turned to my parents, in particular, Dad, for answers. Both passed away many years ago, but their imprint on me remains.

I admire both of my parents greatly, in particular, their courage to forge ahead in support of their values, regardless of the cost. Why have I not been able to muster the courage they have? What has held me back?

This book has allowed me to identify the major life lessons I have learned from Dad and consider how they have shown up in my life.

Perhaps I have displayed as much courage as my parents, but just in different ways and for different reasons.

Throughout the remainder of this book, I will explore five important lessons Dad passed on to me, not deliberately, but through his actions and words.

I encourage you, the reader, to take time to mine your own parents' legacies for life lessons. Whether you maintain close relationships with your parents, have been estranged from them for many years, admire them, or despise them, your parents have taught you lessons, explicitly or not. Capture them, examine them, and figure out their impact on you. The process is freeing, regardless, and you may learn more about the unique being that is you.

A nod to historical and personal veracity

Throughout this book, I have tried my best to be as accurate as possible with historical information that can be easily verified. Ultimately, though, this is a book of memories, both memories of what I was told and memories of what I experienced directly. Consequently, their veracity may not be perfect. However, that really does not matter because this book is about how the lessons I learned from my father showed up in my life, and I am the expert on that.

In addition, I have striven to be honest and forthright about my relationship with Dad and my experiences growing up. Some of you may notice relatively few points of conflict with Dad and wonder whether I may be whitewashing my story. The truth is, I grew up in a remarkably drama-free family. Sure, there were occasional disagreements with Dad, but none I remember with any clarity at this point. They just weren't significant—or frequent—enough. Dad certainly wasn't perfect, but he came pretty darn close.

Chapter Two

Lesson 1 – Art is Essential

"The artist has specific ideas in mind and in representing these ideas in spirit as well as in fact, he chews up the forms with his emotions which leaves a prevailing mood."

~Kemper Nomland, Jr.

I grew up in a work of art. From the diamond chain-shaped structure that supported the roof of the driveway to the Mondrian-styled wall along the bridge leading to the front door, you knew from the start that this was not a cookie-cutter house. When you entered the house, you found yourself at a crossroads overseen by a print of one of Modigliani's long-necked women. You had a choice: Downstairs to the public area or left, right, or center into the bathroom or bedrooms. Regardless of your choice, you were met with light, lots of light, wood, and art.

The house I was born into was a mid-century modern gem that Dad designed to fit perfectly on the last lot on horseshoe-shaped Mavis Drive before the first curve to the left. It stood halfway up the hill on Mt. Washington in Northeast Los Angeles. It was my only home until I set out on my own at the age of 23.

In this chapter, I introduce you to the first lesson I learned from Dad—that art is essential and life-affirming.

An artist at heart

Dad was born an artist. Where that impulse came from is unclear, but I think it was innate. Dad was always creating—in many media—including acrylics, watercolor, pen and ink, print, charcoal, and clay. His styles evolved over time, beginning with realism, moving into more abstract pieces, and ending with a focus on whimsical reptiles.

As a young man just out of high school, Dad attended Pasadena City College, where he studied under George Flower, head of the Art Center Institute, and Virginia Ballard Flower, a noted sculptor. Both Mr. and Mrs. Flower had a profound impact on Dad, inspiring him to select portrait painting and sculpture as his life's work.

Dad's art, though, extended to his graphic design and layout work, his architectural designs, his furniture, and his sumptuous cooking and baking. His Croquembouche and pumpkin cheesecake were to die for, but what I miss most are those Willie-Billies, with their cinnamony goodness and sugary glaze.

Jazz, blues, and rock n' roll

Dad was not a musician. He could not carry a tune to save his life. That probably also explained why he had no facility for learning languages, in contrast to my mother, who spoke several languages fluently.

But what he lacked in innate musical talent, he made up for in his love for music. Dad had an impressive collection of both 78s and 33s— the old school vinyl records that only those of a certain age are familiar with. In his heyday, Dad's favorite genres were jazz, blues, and gospel. The record player was tucked neatly away in a dining room closet—classic Dad. Because the public first-level of the house was an open concept with easy access from the living room to the dining room to the kitchen, having the record player there was ideal.

Up in my room on the second floor, I could enjoy phrasings from the likes of Billie Holiday, Mahalia Jackson, and Lead Belly. To this day, Christmas isn't Christmas without Ella Fitzgerald's jazzy renditions of "Santa Claus Is Coming to Town" with its "it's in the bag" ending and "Rudolph, the Red-Nosed Reindeer" from her classic *Ella Wishes You a Swinging Christmas* album.

Starting in the 1960s, Dad began to add folk, folk-rock, and rock songs to his record list. Pete Seeger, Arlo Guthrie, and Simon and Garfunkel were among his top picks. But when my parents threw a party, it had to include Tom Lehrer's incredibly witty and political album, *That Was the Year That Was*. If you haven't heard Lehrer's "Vatican Rag" or "National Brotherhood Week," stop everything and listen to them!

Dad came to appreciate rock n' roll mostly thanks to me. He was never a Presley or Little Richard fan, but when I came down with the chicken pox at the age of 11, my parents let me select a record album of my choosing as a distraction. My choice was The Beatles' *Sgt. Pepper's Lonely Hearts Club Band.* Dad loved it.

The Fine Arts Group

A seminal period in Dad's life was the time he spent as a conscientious objector during World War II in the Waldport Civilian Public Service (CPS) camp, Camp #56. The role that pacifism played in Dad's life was on par with that of art, and the two were inextricably linked.

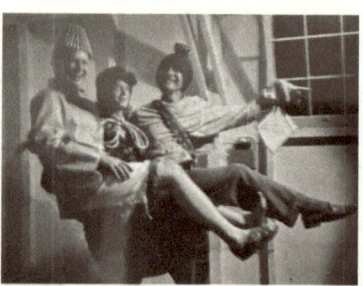

Dad, Manche Langley, and Kermit Sheets at Waldport CPS Camp #56.

To give conscientious objectors educational opportunities to develop skills that could be put to use after the war, the Brethren Church, which oversaw Cascade Locks CPS Camp #21 as well as Waldport CPS Camp #56 (both in Oregon), solicited ideas from internees regarding the sorts of educational programs they would like to see. Dad and his friend, Kermit Sheets, two internees at Camp #21, suggested a fine arts program. After much debate as to the best camp at which to locate such a program, it was decided to house it at Camp #56.

The prospectus for the proposed fine arts program, which would eventually be referred to as the Fine Arts Group, was carefully worded to be as inclusive as possible:

"The Fine Arts School, as we conceive it, is simply to be a grouping together of the practitioners of the various art forms. These include the Literary Arts: fiction, poetry, essays, and criticism; the Musical Arts: both composition and performance; the Visual Arts: painting and sculpture; the Speech Arts: dramatics and readings; and the related fine arts crafts."

It was here in the Fine Arts Group that Dad blossomed as an artist. Feeding off the energy of a group of incredibly talented artists, including poet William Everson, who later became Brother Antoninus, book designer and fine arts printer, Adrian Wilson, who received a 1983 MacArthur "genius grant," poet William Stafford (who served in another camp, but contributed to the Fine Arts Group's publications), and author Henry Miller. Dad's artwork and layout skills took the Group's books to the next level, although the U.S. Postal Service would refuse to deliver them at times because they deemed the content inappropriate or pornographic.

Dad told one story about the cover of *The Illiterati*, which featured the yellow palm of an outstretched hand with a red circle in the middle of the palm. It was one of the publications rejected by the U.S. Postal Service. As Dad told it, "It had a hand and a circle on the hand. So someone decided that the circle represented Japan. Our enemy. It was just a circle as far as I knew."

Every ruin has a story

Have you ever been dragged miles over a mountain pass to see the feet of a statue, the rest of whose body had long since disintegrated? Or foregone lunch in order to reach two stones in a neighboring village that once belonged to the Temple of Artemis? Mom and I were often the unwitting accomplices of Dad, who had boundless energy when it came to visiting ruins of ancient civilizations. For Dad, it was the culmination of an adventure that often began months prior to a trip, during which he read extensively about the history of an area and wanted to experience it firsthand, even when very little of it remained.

Sometimes we complained, like the time when we had just completed a 12-hour flight to Munich, Germany, and picked up a new BMW there. Mom and I were exhausted, but Dad was just hitting his stride. There was just this one archaeological site he had read about only 50 kilometers away. In the end, Dad usually won out because his childlike enthusiasm was infectious.

A marriage of site and structure

In 1945, *Arts and Architecture Magazine* launched the Case Study House Program. The idea behind the program was to encourage architects to design and build homes to house the millions of soldiers returning from World War II. The program was a competition of sorts in which only 36 homes were selected during the program's duration until 1966. To be considered for the program, a home had to exemplify its tenets, which included the following:

- The use of inexpensive and readily available building materials

- Affordability for the average American

- Simple design

- Integration of indoor and outdoor living

Nearly all the homes selected were in and around Los Angeles.

Case Study House #10 was not originally considered for inclusion in the Case Study House Program. It was built in 1947 as the primary residence for Dad's parents. Its expansive open design and connection to the outdoors made it the perfect home for family gatherings. For years, it was the go-to place for holiday celebrations and birthday parties.

Case Study House #10.

Unlike many of the homes selected for the Case Study House Program, Case Study House #10, the only Case Study house in Pasadena, was already built when it was chosen. Although the architects on the house were shown as Nomland and Nomland, Case Study House #10 is all Dad.

Along with many other residential gems in Los Angeles and elsewhere in Southern California, Case Study House #10 cemented Dad's legacy as a mid-century modern architect.

Christmas cards as works of art with a message

When Mom and Dad moved into their Mt. Washington home in 1955, Dad started a new tradition—homemade Christmas cards that reflected both his artistic and literary prowess.

On a few occasions, the cards featured drawings by Dad of me, with or without one of my many pets, and much later, a drawing of his grandson, Kemal. Most of the cards, though, were colorful watercolors or drawings, some with distinctly Christmas themes and others with abstract designs. All had a message. If Dad's literary muse was weary, Dad would opt for a simple "Happy Holidays" or "Happy New Year." But more often than not, inspiration would strike and the result would be magical, as in:

"The dream can happen!
The world a vast mosaic of different
peoples, cultures, lands and creatures
forming a pattern that, with love, can
become a new Eden:
The third Millennium"

On one occasion, when I was 15, Dad invited me to collaborate with him on a card. He provided the image and asked for me to provide the text. It read:

"Bleak future, forewarning past.
How long will your life last, solitary dove?

Senseless ideals, gruesome goals.
Antagonists try to cage you,
But your convictions are too strong.

And may they grow each dawn."

How this lesson guided my life

If Dad had delivered no other lesson to me than the importance of
art in our lives, that would have been enough. Art ignites creativity
and innovation. It makes us happy and alive. It takes us outside
ourselves and gives us the gift of appreciating others. Art gives us
hope and inspires us to do better and be better.

Erika with a Statue.

Growing up, I often wished my artistic abilities rivaled those of Dad's, although he never thought to compare us and always encouraged my artistic expression. This allowed me to find the artistic outlet best suited to me, namely expository and technical writing, as well as poetry.

I had no desire to follow in Dad's footsteps and become an architect. Just as he was able to combine his engineering and artistic aptitudes in his architecture work, I combined my understanding of software and hardware development with writing in my careers as a technical communicator, business analyst, and product manager.

Erika in a Halloween
Costume Designed by Her
Dad.

Thanks to Dad, my life's musical soundtrack has been diverse. I enjoy classical, jazz, folk, disco, and rock n' roll and although it is the music of my youth that resonates most with me, I have discovered many recent songs that touch me deeply, including Alicia Keyes' "Underdog," Linkin Park's "Somewhere I Belong," and Jon Batiste's "Freedom." But I also love my Boston, Santana, and Fleetwood Mac. Unlike Dad, I can carry a tune. And I relished my time as a guitarist.

Chapter Three

Lesson 2 – Discovery Without Play is Not Possible

"At the edge of the sea is our destination – the city of the mind"
~Kemper Nomland, Jr.

"**A**ll work and no play makes Jack a dull boy" was never an admonition that could be directed at Dad. Unlike many in modern American society, Dad understood the importance of play to clear the tangle of thoughts brought on by a 24/7 mentality. Don't get me wrong—Dad worked hard when he needed to and when he wanted to. But climbing the corporate ladder and increasing his power were alien concepts to him. He never aspired to such goals.

Dad did not have a competitive bone in his body. Very occasionally he watched a sports competition, like the Olympics or a basketball game, but he could take it or leave it. In his mind, such events did not constitute play because play, according to Dad's definition, was a noncompetitive activity—a way to relax, have fun, and open the mind to new ideas. Dad never really understood my own attraction to competitive running, although he never objected to my interest in it.

In this chapter, I explore the ways in which Dad used play as a means to discover new and innovative ways to address the challenges of life.

Playing in the dirt

Dad was an avid gardener. He seemed to have an encyclopedic knowledge of plants. He would often tell me the names of plants, even their scientific names, but sadly, that information usually went in one ear and out the other. I marveled at how patient Dad remained when I asked him for the umpteenth time what the name of a particular plant was.

Erika Cooling Off With a Hose.

For Dad, gardening was an extension of his creative impulse. Sweet peas were a favorite of his. Every spring, Dad would reconstruct the lattice-work to support his sweet peas. When they had grown tall enough, he picked a bouquet for the house so that we could enjoy their sensuous, soothing fragrance indoors.

Gardening reinforced Dad's already patient nature. The growth of living things could not be rushed. With his eye for detail, Dad could appreciate the subtle changes each day brought—a new bloom, the emergence of a seedling, and—to his annoyance—the disappearance of a carrot, evidence of a gopher.

Imaginary worlds under the covers

On the weekends, when there was no rush to get ready for work and school, my parents would often linger in bed. It was Dad's routine to prepare what we called "first breakfast," which consisted of coffee and a sweet roll or piece of toast with butter and jam for my parents and some orange juice or milk for me. I joined my parents in their bedroom for "first breakfast," perched on a comfortable chair at the base of their bed.

As a young child, I occasionally had the opportunity to play under their covers once they had cleared the dishes to the tray. My parents would remain in bed with their knees bent to support the book or magazine they were reading. This would create a tent-like area for me to crawl into. Sometimes I would pretend I was in a cave, taking shelter from a storm with an assortment of animals. I felt protected and warm.

A community lot

The neighborhood I grew up in was a planned community, but not in the sense that it had a bunch of lookalike homes designed by a builder for optimal profit. Our neighborhood was a collaboration among a group of friends from diverse backgrounds looking to establish an integrated community. They were lucky among them to have an architect (in Dad) and building-trade representatives, including a carpenter and a plumber. But the best thing about our neighborhood from a child's perspective was the magical playground we called the community lot.

Life on the Community Lot.

The community lot was a plot of land collectively owned by all the folks surrounding it. If you looked up at it from the lower street, Starling Way, you could see it had three parts. On the left was an elevated area about the size of a large master bedroom. There stood a rickety swing set shadowed by a disheveled sycamore tree. In the middle of the lot was a tennis court-sized section that was just dirt. And on the right was a magnificent playhouse and a sandpit. As a child, I frequently led (bossed around) the other neighborhood kids in games and adventure—Avis, Gary, April, and the Martin children. For some reason, the Moore children near Starling Way's dead-end rarely joined us. During the summer, we whiled away the long days on the community lot until our parents yelled up or down for us to come home for dinner.

Evening board games

Our family game was Scrabble and Mom was the Queen. Dad and I went along, but knew full well that we would likely lose. Mom had the superior English vocabulary, despite the fact that it was her second language. Plus, we always played at Mom's desk, which gave her a distinct advantage because she had the comfortable spot on the left side of the desk with plenty of legroom. We, on the other hand, had to pull up chairs from elsewhere in the room and turn sideways to be close enough to reach the board.

Where Dad shined was when we played *with* dominos. Notice that I said "played *with* dominos" (not played dominos). We never played dominos, but we liked to line up the pieces in different configurations and then start the chain reaction. Dad was a builder, so he knew instinctively how to position the dominos for optimal effect. Mom, by the way, never partook of playing *with* dominos. That was not her forte.

Quiet time

In retrospect, I realize how fortunate I was to have grown up in a household that cherished calm and order. Every day there were long periods during which silence prevailed. Ours was a very cerebral home. Both my parents and I devoted a lot of time to quiet study, play, and creation. That being said, we still had fun together, lively conversations, and TV time.

Erika with Her Toys During Quiet Time.

Each weekend afternoon, particularly as a young child, quiet time was enforced. Mom and Dad would retire to their bedroom for an hour or two, during which they expected me to entertain myself. It was excellent training, instilling in me the importance of learning to enjoy alone time. I usually spent the time playing with my toys, building structures with blocks, and conversing with imaginary characters. I gave no thought to what Mom and Dad might be doing, although, as an adult, I have my ideas.

The studio

When Dad designed our Mt. Washington family home, it was a two-story house, with the entry on the second level. Over time, though, Dad yearned for a creative space for himself, and so the studio was born. Dad designed the studio to fit compactly under the first story of the house, with a view of the canyon. The studio enabled Dad to leave out projects in various stages of completion. It was also large enough to house his printer—think Gutenberg, not Hewlett-Packard. Dad mostly used his printing press for the family Christmas cards, but occasionally, he printed newsletters and invitations to events. Besides the printing press itself, the studio was occupied by a large drafting table, where he frequently created or revised architectural drawings, an enormous sink, a toilet stall, and a cabinet with multiple drawers for typefaces of many styles, serif and sans serif alike.

The studio was only accessible from the outside. There was no access to the main house. If it was raining, it meant getting dressed for the elements before making the trek into the backyard and getting your shoes muddy along the unpaved portion of the path. This was both a disadvantage and an advantage. The advantage was that Dad was less likely to be interrupted unless it was absolutely necessary. At times, Dad would spend hours in the studio designing our next Christmas card. On those days, we looked forward to seeing the prototype that resulted.

How this lesson guided my life

Above all, this lesson—that discovery is not possible without play—taught me respect for the creative process, an essential step of which is play, unstructured time to have fun, let the mind wander, and just be.

Erika Taking a Break
During Family Travels in
Europe.

I appreciate the creative spark that ignites when I take a shower, go on a long walk, or drift off to sleep. I have learned to have pen and paper (or smartphone) nearby to jot down ideas before they disappear as quickly as they came.

Although I have never been drawn to gardening, I marvel at the animal life in the garden. I delight in the antics of the squirrels, the social skills of the crows, and the occasional caterpillar that chooses our house as the site for its metamorphosis. That began as a child on the hill, where a wider assortment of animals entered my sphere, from walking sticks to tarantulas to great horned owls and raccoons.

I was often the instigator of group activities on the community lot and beyond. I would begin by describing the vision—first we would do this, then we would do that. There were chase scenes, travel caravans, and treks into the wilderness. I am certain this is where my leadership training began, although I saw my role back then as the creator of fun.

Finally, this lesson gave me an appreciation of alone time to refresh the mind and body before reentering the hustle that is life in the big city.

Chapter Four

Lesson 3 – Your Values Have No Offramps

From "Is There No Way"

Is there no way
but to kill for life
must it always be hate to love
oppress for freedom
starve for plenty
can there be no peace
till all people are straitjacketed
into the stunting way of the one who
possesses the violence of victory
till all shall conform under continuous
coercion of steel
and threat of steel
must the chaos of compulsion

the rigid ring of wrath
and might be the measure of right
can we only be kind after conquering
must I bury a man
before he can be my brother?
~Kemper Nomland, Jr.
The Illiterati, Number Three
(Waldport, Oregon: Untide Press, Summer 1944)

T he household I grew up in was a free-flowing switchboard of ideas. No topics were off-limits. But that was not true of behaviors. That you conducted yourself with integrity, responsibility, and respect was non-negotiable. Both Mom and Dad set the bar high, and they expected me to measure up. What I soon learned was that doing so was the key to happiness, not in the sense that it allowed me to avoid punishment, but rather that it gave me peace of mind.

Dad's stands against injustice and violence as a means of settling disputes were unshakeable because of his commitment to integrity, responsibility, and respect. Once he dedicated himself to a cause he believed in, he spoke out forthrightly and consistently, and he accepted the responsibility that came with taking a stand. He also treated others with respect, even when their beliefs were contrary to his own. However, he did not shy away from speaking his truth.

In this chapter, I offer Dad's life as one roadmap for living in accordance with your values, even when doing so creates hardships.

Risking disdain

When Dad received his draft notice after the U.S.'s entry into World War II, he knew he could not participate in the war effort. Initially, he thought the Congregational Church of which he was a member would support him in his decision based on the teachings of Christ. But that is not what happened. The Church had no interest in his ideas. Undeterred, Dad went to the draft board to apply for a 4-E classification (conscientious objector opposed to both combatant and noncombatant training and service). Although his Church had not supported his decision to register as a conscientious objector, he told the draft board that he had made his decision based on what he had learned at church. The classification was granted and Dad was sent to the first of two Civilian Public Service (CPS) camps for the duration of the war.

Dad, Don Baker, and Kermit Sheets.

Being a conscientious objector in "The Good War," though, had its price. According to some members of CPS Camp #56, the residents in nearby Waldport "hated" them. During their forays into town, camp members were often subjected to disdainful looks and mean comments. The local newspaper frequently published hateful articles about the camp that were filled with falsehoods and malicious propaganda. In an ironic twist, the printing machine that the editor of the local newspaper had given permission to sell was sold to members of the Fine Arts Group at Camp #56.

Risking arrest

Not long before the end of World War II, Dad staged a work slowdown. Much of the work Dad and others did as part of Camp #56 was done under the auspices of the U.S. Forest Service. That included downing timber and clearing trails. As Dad's productivity came to a standstill, the Forest Service became frustrated and began refusing to let him join in the work.

Eventually, Dad was arrested. As the story goes, Dad was then escorted by two government officials to Portland, Oregon, where he was to be arraigned. On the way, the officials stopped at a bar for a few drinks, presumably leaving Dad secured in the car. When they returned, it was too late to complete the trip to Portland, so they got a hotel room, with the plan to continue the journey the next day. The next day, as luck would have it, the war ended, so the arraignment never happened. Dad served a short time on probation, but that was it.

Risking rejection

As a nonconformist, Dad rarely chose the Easy button. His values and beliefs were his anchors and they were often at odds with the prevailing national mood. When asked how he had helped the war effort, he did not have an acceptable soldier story. When asked where he lived and who his neighbors were, he could not satisfy those who chose their neighbors based on their skin color.

Any rejection Dad faced, though, didn't phase him because for him, it wasn't important. As long as he honored his values, he felt secure.

Encouraging resistance

Unless the status quo respected human life and promoted fairness and equality, Dad resisted it. He often took me to marches—against the war du jour, in favor of fair housing, and in support of civil rights. I learned quickly to appreciate the power an individual can wield in a democracy. In high school, two friends and I staged our own march at the corner of Avenue 45 and Figueroa in Northeast Los Angeles to draw attention to our environment and the need to clean up our air and water, long before "climate change" was part of the vernacular.

Dad's resistance to the draft may have begun with his own situation, but when another big war rolled around in the form of the Vietnam War, Dad dusted off his resistance boots and started walking. In his 80s, Dad was still out there in front of Leisure World with homemade signs and his now scratchy voice to object to the Iraqi War and the continuing arms race.

Encouraging creation

Whether in his gardening, his baking, his art, or his architecture, Dad was all about encouraging the creative force within us. The guiding principle of *The Illiterati*, the magazine Dad and others created at CPS Camp #56, was "that all organisms form an interconnected whole, that separation is possible only on the mental or verbal levels, and that war and all forms of physical coercion are always destructive of man." This principle speaks to creation in its broadest interpretation.

*Dad With His Painting
of Kermit Sheets.*

Ultimately, creation was the driving philosophy in Dad's life. Everything Dad did was about honoring creation and creativity.

Encouraging belonging

When your view of humans is at the character level, stripped of the artifices of race, ethnic background, national affiliation, and religion, belonging is a given, as long as your character measures up. That was Dad's view of the world. He cared only that his neighbors and friends were good people—kind, respectful, curious, open-minded, and supportive. Perhaps in part to remind himself that character was everything, Dad enjoyed and celebrated the diversity of the world and surrounded himself with it.

He encouraged belonging by creating a diverse neighborhood at a time when such neighborhoods were rare. There is no doubt I was raised by the Mt. Washington neighborhood I grew up in. I ate many meals in the homes of neighbors who graciously included me in their lunch or dinner plans. Every summer, the Scotts, an older black couple with the only swimming pool in the area, invited us to spend the summer in their pool. It was glorious!

How this lesson guided my life

Despite being inoculated many times over the years with an anti-hypocrisy vaccine, mustering the strength of character to stand up for my convictions has not always been easy, particularly as a child and young adult. During those formative years, I often felt as though I did not belong. Not only were my parents outspoken, they were also older than most of my friends' parents and were, at times, mistaken for my grandparents. I just wanted to fit in, and those realities ran contrary to that need.

With age, though, I have come to appreciate this lesson most of all and the courage it takes to embrace one's values and never discard them for expediency. Although I have not always taken on the big issues Dad did, I have not shied away from speaking up for those unable to speak up for themselves without jeopardizing their livelihood, security, or health. At work, I have defended those who were attacked or bullied. In one instance, a colleague from India who worked remotely was being driven to work excessive hours by a contract project manager. When the colleague sent me an email that lacked coherence, I knew I had to speak up. I emailed the project manager and forcefully told her to give my colleague a few days off. She never responded directly to me, but shortly after I sent my email, she notified the team that my colleague would be away from the office for a few days.

More recently, I have come to a greater appreciation of the importance of making people feel as though they belong. After the need for food, water, and shelter, the need to belong is critical to one's well-being. Whether you are an immigrant, a traveller, or a member of an underserved community, you have likely struggled with the feeling that you don't belong. When Dad agreed to sponsor the man I loved and wanted to marry, sight unseen, from a very different culture and background, the beauty in making people feel they belong became clear.

Chapter Five

Lesson 4 – Peace is Always an Option

"For peace to flower there can be no enemies"

~Kemper Nomland, Jr.

I n addition to art, pacifism was a prominent thread throughout Dad's life. Unlike art, though, Dad's adherence to his pacifist beliefs led him down paths he likely never imagined as a young man. When that initial spark was lit that caused Dad to embrace a life dedicated to pacifism is anyone's guess. Dad was born in 1919 at the end of the First World War, during which over 116,000 U.S. soldiers lost their lives. It was also at the tail end of the Spanish flu pandemic. Death hung heavy in the air when Dad entered the world and perhaps that fact planted in him a drive to preserve and honor life above all.

Sadly, "the war to end all wars" was not an accurate moniker for World War I. Less than 20 years later, the world was embroiled in another widespread conflict, followed by the Korean War, and then the long-running Vietnam War. The Vietnam War was the first war during which I came to admire Dad, the pacifist. Not long after my eighth birthday, the U.S. entered the Vietnam War. I distinctly remember watching the CBS Evening News with Walter Cronkite during that time. For years, starting in 1965, the broadcast began with a tally of the war dead.

In this chapter, I illustrate the many ways in which Dad's commitment to peace and nonviolence showed up in his life and, subsequently, in mine.

War is not an option

In an interview Dad gave in 2002, in his early 80s, he was asked why he became a conscientious objector. His response was direct and simple: "I could never be involved in killing anybody. I couldn't see any reason for war either. That was the outcome of war, and I just couldn't participate."

When Dad transferred to CPS Camp #56 in Waldport, Oregon to join the Fine Arts Group, he helped to fashion the Group under three distinctive beliefs, along with other members, including poet William Everson, who served as the Group's first director. Those beliefs were captured by the Group in the following words:

1. The widespread destruction of the Second World War was the inevitable result of modern nationalism.

2. The emergence of a mass culture and modern nationalism had eroded human potential by eliminating alternate ways of being in the world.

3. New modes of collective life were needed that were not tied to a wartime culture and the formation of dutiful national subjects.

The breadth of these beliefs and the extent to which they still resonate today are quite remarkable. Once again, war rages in Europe and extreme nationalism is still the instigator.

A life taken does not justify a life taken

Dad's dedication to pacifism and search for nonviolent solutions extended far beyond the purview of war. He believed strongly that "an eye for an eye" approach to meting out justice only left countless blind people in its wake. There was no justification for exacting another life for a life already taken.

Dad was a vocal opponent of the death penalty and used his voice to advocate for its abolition. Although he abhorred the killing of a fellow human being, he felt that life in prison and a loss of freedom was a sufficient price to pay.

Guns have no place in our world

Not surprisingly, Dad never owned a gun. Thinking back over my childhood and young adult years, I never saw a real gun except on police officers and then only in their holsters. Other than that, guns were only props in films and stage productions.

I was in my teens when the reality of gun violence hit home. A good friend of my father's and a fellow conscientious objector, George Maurer, was shot by an intruder who was looking to burglarize the home George was house sitting. For many years, George lived at the bottom of Mt. Washington at the corner of Avenue 45 and Glenalbyn Drive. He held a special place in my heart because every year as far back as I could remember, he gifted me a German advent calendar to count down the days to Christmas Eve. To this day, I buy an advent calendar every season and think of him.

Dad with Friends at Cascade Locks Camp #21, including George Maurer (second from the left).

Later in life, Dad regularly supported anti-gun organizations, such as the National Coalition to Ban Handguns.

Alternatives to war

One of Dad's biggest concerns was the country's military-industrial complex. The vast sums of money spent on bolstering the military and developing more and more deadly ways of killing each other meant far less money spent on quality-of-life issues, such as poverty, education, and housing. Dad paid his taxes, fair and square, but lamented the fact that they were not always spent the way he would have spent them. Dad saw engagement in the political process as one important approach to altering this trajectory. Voting was not just a right; it was an obligation.

Having himself been a conscientious objector, Dad felt it was necessary to give back and mentor future conscientious objectors, most of whom were looking for alternatives to serving in combatant and noncombatant roles as part of the ongoing conflict in Vietnam. Dad found joy in this activity, but rejoiced when the draft was abolished in 1973. To quote from a flyer Dad printed called "Don't Register for World War 3": "We must obey the law or take the consequences. But when a law runs so counter to the traditions of democracy and freedom of individual conscience as does a peacetime draft, the danger of obeying may be greater to the nation than the danger of disobeying to a few."

Respect for the peacemakers

Dad surrounded himself with peacemakers. Many of his closest friends were those he met during the Second World War while he served time in CPS camps. Particularly the men in the Fine Arts Group, with whom he also shared a love for the arts, became lifelong friends. With these men, he felt a special kinship.

Many of his peacemaker friends settled in San Francisco after the war, where a burgeoning counterculture movement was taking hold and where they were instrumental in shaping the Beat poetry of the 1950s. As a child, I accompanied my parents on frequent trips to the Bay Area and even to Portland, Oregon for occasional CPS camp reunions. Some of Dad's friends became my friends, whom my husband and I visited in later years.

One of Dad's peacemaker friends was Glenn Smiley, the minister who married my husband and me. After the war, Smiley became one of Martin Luther King, Jr.'s closest advisors and was largely responsible for King's adoption of nonviolent resistance. According to Raymond Arsenault, author of *Freedom Riders: 1961 and the Struggle for Racial Justice*, "Smiley had a profound influence on King's pilgrimage to nonviolence. When King took the first integrated bus ride following the boycott's successful conclusion in December 1956, he fittingly gave Smiley the honor of sitting by his side."

My Wedding Officiated by
Glenn Smiley.

Among Dad's heroes were Mahatma Gandhi and Martin Luther King, Jr., both of whom showed the world what nonviolent resistance could accomplish.

Civil disobedience

Civil disobedience, a term coined by poet and essayist Henry David Thoreau in his piece, *Resistance to Civil Government*, was what Dad engaged in when he decided to stage a work slowdown at the end of his internment in CPS Camp #56, which signaled that he could no longer abide by the alternative service he had earlier accepted.

Not all conscientious objectors agreed to the terms of the draft board's E-4 classification. Technically, accepting those terms did not constitute civil disobedience. Some such conscientious objectors spent time in prison. One organization Dad supported was the Resist Conscription Committee, or RCC, with offices in Los Angeles and New York. The RCC encouraged "conscientious civil disobedience... until the draft is repealed." Dad participated in protests organized by the RCC, cultivating civil disobedience as the appropriate response to a mandatory draft.

How this lesson guided my life

As a woman coming of age when I did, I was fortunate not to face the weighty decisions Dad had to tackle as a young man. Yet, in retrospect, it is clear that Dad's commitment to pacifism impacted me directly.

Twice, early in my career, I turned down and left jobs because they took on military contracts that they expected me to participate in. In one case, a team I was part of worked past midnight to complete a Request for Proposal (RFP) that would have involved the manufacture of bombs. I cried all the way home and vowed to look for a new job. A month later, I submitted my resignation.

As a lifelong animal lover, I have chosen to focus my own pacifism on our animal family, a path that has continued to evolve. Several years ago, I chose to give up all mammal meat, including (but not limited to) pork, beef, and lamb. I also make a point of capturing as many as possible of the smaller critters (insects and spiders—even cockroaches) that occasionally take refuge in our home and placing them back outside. I remind myself that they have as much right to be here on earth as I do.

I am buoyed by efforts to abolish the death penalty and limit the proliferation of firearms. I wish that no one felt the need to possess guns of any kind, except perhaps for the purpose of competitive shooting, but I remain more of a realist than Dad, for whom many issues were all-or-nothing propositions.

Finally, I try my best to be patient with people, secure in the knowledge that on those rare occasions when someone lashes out at me, their behavior is usually not related to anything I did. I have learned to respond calmly and kindly. Calm and kindness have much to recommend them.

Chapter Six

Lesson 5 – Justice is All or Nothing

"The mosaic of our diversity is our humanity."
~Kemper Nomland, Jr.

"I magine all the people sharing all the world" is just one of many lines in John Lennon's classic, *Imagine*, that make it the perfect anthem for Dad's life. Dad believed strongly in "a brotherhood of man" and although he was a dreamer, he put his dreams into action. Exploring the world in all its magnificent diversity was one of Dad's passions, whether that meant experiencing other cultures first hand or through an exhibit at a museum or local gallery.

Despite the inconveniences brought on by a world built on nationalism, Dad forged ahead, eager to immerse himself in all the shades of life. Dad never considered who might be more deserving of privilege than another. Such a concept was foreign to him. That people might be treated differently based on their physical characteristics or place of birth made no sense to him. But just as he had learned to use his voice to wage war on war, he learned to apply the same tactics to fight injustice.

In this chapter, I describe Dad's belief that our personal actions make a difference and that the American experiment, even with its flaws, demands we take an active role in making it a more perfect union. I also show the many ways in which Dad sought to embrace and respect all life on earth—and indeed the earth itself. He believed strongly in the "live and let live" mantra, that all people should have an equal opportunity to pursue their dreams. I am grateful that he passed on this lesson to me, although it materialized differently for me than for him.

Harnessing the democratic process

Mine was a political household. Dad was a life-long Democrat, always on the liberal end of the spectrum. His actions made it clear that he had a deep respect for our democracy and our responsibility as informed voters. When election time rolled around, Dad would do his homework. He studied the stands of each candidate, attended local candidate forums, and read the fine print of each proposition. Dad was a member of the local Democratic club and rarely missed a meeting, particularly during an election cycle.

On election day, I frequently accompanied my parents to the polls. Voting in person on election day was the only option back then. Seeing my parents vote and Dad's prep leading up to election day drove home the importance of voting. When I turned 18 on November 3, 1974, I had just two days to wait until the midterm elections on November 5. I took my role as a newly minted voter very seriously. Prior to the election, I spent the better part of a day at the Los Angeles Downtown Library researching all the propositions and candidates before marking my sample ballot. I have to admit I have not been as conscientious in my research since then, but I still allot time to figuring out my ballot choices before voting.

Dad not only made sure he was ready to vote, he also made sure his fellow Angelenos were ready to vote. In the weeks leading up to an election, Dad could often be found at the local grocery store or library manning a registration table and using his persuasive skills to encourage others to vote.

Banishing otherness

One of my favorite quotes of Dad's is the following:
"The dream can happen!
The world a vast mosaic of different
people, cultures, lands and creatures
forming a pattern that, with love, can
become a new Eden:
The third Millennium"
It summed up his belief that people should be evaluated based solely on the merits of their character. Was a person kind, honest, open-minded, and respectful? For Dad, a person's culture and language were embellishments to be understood and, in many cases, celebrated. One thing that strikes me about this quote is the absence of any mention of nations. A nation remained a fraught concept for Dad because it came with the inevitable baggage of

"mine and yours," which all too often meant having to defend what was mine.

Dad always looked for ways to bring people to the table, or to join tables he might not otherwise have been part of. Dad was not a religious man; he referred to himself as an agnostic. Yet Dad loved to learn about various religious traditions and visit churches, cathedrals, mosques, and synagogues, in part because these places of worship were often some of the most beautiful, innovative, and striking architectural examples in any given town or city. He even designed a church himself—the Norwegian Seamen's Church of San Pedro, California.

Dad relished participating in the Posadas Navideñas during a 1994 visit to his brother and sister-in-law in Dolores Hidalgo, Mexico and a Rosh Hashanah seder meal in Los Angeles in the 1970s, to which I accompanied him, but he equally enjoyed bringing together people from diverse backgrounds to break bread in his own home. Guests routinely represented a kaleidoscope of races, cultures, and religions. Such gatherings brought Dad great joy.

Posadas Navideñas in Dolores Hidalgo.

Travel as a gateway to understanding

Like his father before him, Dad loved to travel. During his lifetime, Dad traveled extensively in the United States, Canada, Mexico, and Europe. I have no doubt that he would have loved to travel in Asia, South America, and Africa, but time got away from him. Dad was the opposite of an "ugly American." Immersing himself in the city life, food, culture, and art of a place made him happy. During our first visit to Turkey after I married my Turkish husband, Erol, Dad was like a kid in a candy shop. In Istanbul, he and Erol experienced a traditional Turkish bath, as did I (in a separate bathhouse, of course) and savored half a barbecued lamb's head (an image that has always made me cringe).

When I was five years old, my parents decided we would live abroad for half a year. With a base camp in Kiel, Germany, Mom's hometown, we traveled extensively throughout Europe, visiting many spots I have yet to return to as an adult. This adventure started with a bang. Upon our arrival in Germany, Dad was hit with an acute appendicitis that required he be hospitalized and undergo surgery. Thankfully, Mom was there to facilitate communication. With youth (Dad was 43 at the time) and otherwise good health on his side, Dad recovered quickly, taking it all in stride and choosing to frame the experience as yet another travel story. Living in Europe for six months gave us the opportunity to appreciate the many cultures of Europe, from England to Portugal to Sweden and Greece—and many points in between. Sadly, I only have a few memories from that time, but they are overwhelmingly positive, including my first gondola ride in Venice, my first sips of wine (heavily diluted), my Dutch girl hat, which I wore incessantly, and a chance encounter with a group of young Greek women in Athens, who were intrigued with the little American girl.

One of our most memorable trips to Europe included a foray into East Germany, which required careful planning, including securing visas. I was a young teenager during that first trip, which I likened to a journey from a world of color (in West Germany) to a world of black and white. Buildings that were only a few years old looked ancient and decrepit. We made sure we had nothing in our possession that might be considered controversial. East Germany's initial draw for us were two of Mom's dearest friends from childhood, Annemarie and Hedwig, whom she had maintained contact with, despite their being on the east side of the wall when it went up. For all of us, though, it was a fascinating entrée into a closed society in which personal freedoms were severely curtailed. Also striking about East Germany were the many ruins left from the Second World War, many previously magnificent structures, such as the Zwinger and Frauenkirche in Dresden. Our appreciation for our life back in the States was bolstered significantly by the experience.

Erika as a Teenager in
Amsterdam.

Travel afforded Dad—indeed all of us—the opportunity to experience new worlds that reinforced all that we share as humans, while allowing him to marvel at the diverse perspectives we humans are capable of. Recently, I was given the original college recommendation letter written by my high-school counselor. In it, I was surprised to find a paragraph devoted to my parents. In that paragraph, my counselor mentions the following: "Erika is the only child in the family and received many enriching experiences from her family such as the opportunity to have traveled extensively in Europe."

Protest as patriotism

For Dad, protest was always one of the best examples of patriotism. In contrast to the expression "America—love it or leave it," which became popular during the 1960s, Dad's view was that those who truly loved their country wanted it to live up to its potential as a bulwark of democracy and equal opportunity. The Constitution's First Amendment, which guarantees the right to peaceful assembly, was designed as a vehicle for doing just that—speaking up to ensure that the country was on the right track.

Time and again, Dad joined protests against war, unfair housing practices, and civil rights violations. Along with millions of other Americans, Dad saw the fruits of his time spent on the streets in protest. Soldiers were brought home from ill-begotten wars, laws were enacted to guard against unfair housing practices, and in 1964, President Johnson signed into law the Civil Rights Act.

Living with diversity

In the mid-1950s, when segregation was the norm, Dad opted for a different path. When Mom and Dad first got married, they rented a house on Mt. Washington, just one hill over from where they built the home I grew up in. Back in the early 1950s, there was only a smattering of houses up on the hill. Being an architect, Dad knew he would design the family home that he and Mom would live in for most of the rest of their lives. They also had a vision—to build not just a home, but a community. Before long, they had assembled a diverse group of friends and acquaintances who were interested in making Mt. Washington their home.

The Nomland Family Home on
Mt. Washington

Some were friends of Dad's from his CPS camp experience. Others were friends of Mom's. And still others were friends of friends who jumped at the opportunity to explore a new paradigm—an integrated community.

Dad knew from his experiences growing up in Altadena and Pasadena and during the war that the more diverse the community you grew up in, the more likely you were to feel comfortable with a variety of neighbors. It gave you the chance to get to know people as people, stripped of their labels. It convinced you that justice was an all-or-nothing proposition.

Respect for all creatures

One of my favorite stories of Dad and our animal friends happened while I was still in Mom's womb. Dad had hired someone to help him with a big gardening project in the backyard when suddenly he heard a lot of commotion from the other end of the yard where his helper was working. Dad ran over to see what was going on, only to discover that the helper had bludgeoned to death a gopher snake. It was one of the few times when Dad made his anger and disappointment known. The helper had killed the snake to prevent Mom from accidentally seeing it and having a miscarriage. Dad, on the other hand, didn't believe in such superstitions and was upset that one of his best tools for curbing the gopher population was now dead.

Dad instilled in me a love for all of earth's creatures—great and small. Undoubtedly in part because I was an only child, animals of various shapes and sizes became my siblings. Dad realized early on the important role animals could play in my life because he, himself, was an animal lover and had grown up with various pets. Mom, on the other hand, had no experience with pets and was not keen on welcoming them into our home. But thankfully, Dad worked his magic and convinced her to open what later became floodgates. At the height of my animal mania, I had two cats, one dog, chickens, a hamster, and a rabbit.

My first pet was Big Kitty, a rescue from the Pasadena Humane Society with fluffy white fur and one blue eye and one brown eye. She was a very chill cat who put up with a lot from me. I loved to put her in a bonnet, tuck her under the covers in my baby buggy, and wheel her around my room, pretending she was my baby, which, of course, she was. She would usually tolerate the ordeal for about 10 minutes, after which she would shake off the bonnet and jump down.

Erika with Big Kitty.

My love of animals was not confined to the domesticated variety. I was also intrigued with the wild animals that frequented our garden, especially the spiders. During the summer, when the harlequin beetles were in abundance, I enjoyed feeding the hungry spiders who waited patiently for an unsuspecting insect to stumble onto their webs. Rather than leave that to chance, I helped by scooping up a harlequin beetle and dropping it onto a spider's web. That would set off a chain reaction culminating in the beetle being wrapped in web silk for later consumption.

How this lesson guided my life

In some ways, this lesson has impacted me more than the others. It continues to be front and center in many of the activities I choose to spend time on now that I am retired.

Politics and the importance of upholding and strengthening our democratic ideals is a passion of mine. Some might call me a political junkie. Thankfully, I have friends and relatives who help support my habit. I know how essential it is that we have representatives who understand their role and are genuinely doing the job for the right reasons.

When we as women can express ourselves clearly, honestly, and in a compelling voice, we find our strength and confidence. Banishing otherness extends to the circumstances we are cast into because of trauma and health issues. Mental health challenges, just like any other health challenges, are those to be tackled, managed, and hopefully, overcome. These are areas where I have striven to make a difference. Ultimately, my goal is to make us all think twice about labeling people. Labeling only diminishes people's worth and potential. I am thrilled when I throw a stereotypical blanket on someone only to have them toss it aside and show me otherwise.

Thankfully, Dad passed on to me the travel bug. Although perhaps not quite as adventurous as Dad, I learned the benefits of traveling alone to boost your confidence and reliance on yourself. From my travels with my parents, to my first solo trip abroad just out of college, to my many travels since with my own family, I have found in traveling a shortcut to appreciating both our diversity and sameness as citizens of this world.

Last, but certainly not least, I continue to have the greatest respect for all living creatures, their intelligence, kindness, adaptability, and wonder. Having animals in my daily life is necessary. Animals keep me healthy—both physically and mentally. They bring me joy and delight. As my husband says, "they are part of the package!"

Chapter Seven

Reflecting on the Lessons I've Learned

"In younger days when hope was as common as ants in summer
I dismissed dancing as unnecessary, even frivolous.
It was sowing season with no time to waste."
~From *Spotlights of Hope* by Erika Nomland Cilengir

T here comes a time when the pull of the past overrides the immediacy of the present, when it is time to be still and let connections form and insights blossom. It is still sowing season, but of a different kind.

When I embarked on this project, I had no idea that it had been waiting for me to arrive. Dad was often on my mind, particularly because I was always being introduced to new aspects of his life. Random people would contact me because they lived in a house Dad designed and wanted to learn more about him. The author of a book on actress Jane Russell emailed me to say she had become so intrigued by the house Dad designed for Ms. Russell that she devoted an entire chapter of her book to it. A Colorado woman wrote to let me know that Dad's paternal grandparents were founding members of a Lutheran church in North Dakota. And so it goes.

The time was ripe to mine the lessons Dad had given me over the course of his life. Identifying the five lessons in this book was relatively easy, but grasping the impact those lessons had on me was more challenging. Some lessons could be taken at face value; others required more digging. And then there were the ancillary lessons derived from the primary ones, which, in my case, I took as negative lessons. They often proved to be as important as the primary ones.

Here are my main takeaways from these five primary lessons:

Lesson 1—Art is Essential—The creative impulse is not something restricted to the arts, such as painting, music, or acting. The creative impulse can be applied to all our endeavors, including expository and technical writing.

Lesson 2—Discovery Without Play is Not Possible— Making time to play and do nothing is essential to innovating, discovering, and finding that spark that can change everything. You should never feel guilty for taking time to just be and think.

Lesson 3—Your Values Have No Offramps—Despite the risks—at times to life and limb—that sometimes come with standing up for our values, not to stand up for our values is a much greater risk in the long haul because relinquishing our values means giving up on an essential part of who we are. This, in turn, leaves us a soulless shadow of ourselves.

Lesson 4—Peace is Always an Option—Patience is a prerequisite to peace. When faced with conflict, opt for the road to understanding. A calm and measured approach can mean the difference between life and death. Don't take things personally; more often than not, an attack on you is really an attempt to redirect an attack on self.

Lesson 5—Justice is All or Nothing—Stay engaged in your community, venture out into the world, and connect with people from different backgrounds and experiences. More than anything, this teaches you the importance that everyone has the opportunity to pursue their dreams and be treated with respect.

Then, there are the ancillary lessons. In my case, these were lessons I construed negatively as a child and I am continuing to unlearn.

Do not make waves—Growing up with a strong father committed to his values did have a downside for me as a child just wanting to fit in. At times, Dad and Mom, too, would speak out in defense of fairness, but in my child's mind, they were just making trouble, and that cast a shadow on me. I understand how the child version of me felt. Thankfully, as an adult, I no longer feel that way.

Do not stand out—Dad couldn't help but stand out. He was a maverick! He spoke his mind when he needed to—and he was older than most of my friends' fathers. He often even dressed differently, drawn as he was to men's tops from Guatemala. As an adult, I have celebrated these distinctive characteristics. But as a child who wanted to belong and NOT stand out, doing so was much more difficult.

Do not be vulnerable—The northern European stock from which my parents came precluded them from expressing a range of emotions. Only when Mom passed away did I, for a moment, witness Dad crying. For the most part, Dad was stoic and reserved when it came to handling sadness. This was inadvertently conveyed to me. I have spent the better part of my life staving off vulnerability, only recently discovering that vulnerability is a gift.

Honoring the lesson givers

Throughout our lives, we receive lessons, mostly by example. In the beginning, these lessons are usually delivered via our parents or primary caregivers. The ways in which we perceive lessons generally fall into four categories:

1. Positive lessons taken as positive lessons

2. Positive lessons taken as negative lessons

3. Negative lessons taken as negative lessons

4. Negative lessons taken as positive lessons

As I have illustrated throughout this book, the lessons from my father were overwhelmingly positive and, for the most part, I interpreted them as such in my own life. But as I outlined earlier, some of the conclusions I drew from Dad's lessons were detrimental to my growth and development. Those are conclusions I still work to expel from my psyche.

Regardless of the lessons you have received and whether they were positive or negative, take time to acknowledge and honor those who delivered them. That may sound odd if the lessons were negative, but they molded you into the person you are, warts and all. Even negative lessons can be taken in a positive light and lead to miraculous outcomes.

Owning our lessons

Ultimately, we own our lessons. It is up to us to make of them what we will, discarding some and retaining others. Most importantly, we are not prisoners of the lessons handed down to us, whether they are lessons explicitly expressed or modeled in behavior. Remember, we have the ability to put a positive spin on a negative lesson.

Examining the lessons we have learned during the course of our lives and how we have chosen to interpret those lessons can be the key to understanding ourselves better. When I consider the arc of my professional career, I am reminded of lessons I have learned from colleagues and managers along the way that led me to approach problem-solving, advancement, and work relationships in a particular way.

Owning our lessons is just that. It is not about casting blame on those who delivered the lessons. It is about taking stock of what we chose to do with those lessons and why. It is an exercise I recommend to everyone.

Casting away the shadow

I titled this book "In the *shadow* of a maverick" for a reason. For most of my life, Dad's legacy (indeed, the legacies of both of my parents) has weighed heavily on me. I am very proud of all they accomplished in spite of the hurdles thrown in their paths. And yet, I have always felt that my accomplishments did not measure up, that I should have accomplished even more, given a path void of any major hurdles.

What I have come to realize is that the feeling that I have lived my life in Dad's shadow is a myth of my own creation. I am only living my life in another's shadow if I say I am. I must convince myself to the contrary and learn how to be my own inspiration. My journey is distinctly my own to fashion and the things I have accomplished are no better or worse than those of Dad's or anyone else's. The question to ask yourself is: Did I inspire myself today? If the answer is yes, you are on the right path.

Final thoughts

I hope you enjoyed accompanying me on this journey of discovery. Now it is your turn. Whether you focus on one person in your life or several, you are sure to discover things about them—and you—that you never imagined. Although I embarked on this trip later in life, it is a worthwhile exercise at any point. In fact, assessing the lessons you have learned and from whom at various stages gives you the opportunity to make adjustments along the way and get the most from those lessons, whether they are from your father, your mother, or any other pivotal figure in your life.

So, set aside some quiet time and enjoy the journey!

Acknowledgments

This was a book I didn't know I needed to write. Yet sometimes in life we look through the obvious because it is too personal, too painful, too unsettling, or too difficult. This book forced me to confront the obvious head on and revel in its wonder. While creation may be a solitary endeavor at times, it is built on the shoulders of the communities to which we belong.

First, I would like to thank my remarkable parents, Ella and Kemper Nomland, Jr., who gave me a strong foundation and were my primary cheerleaders through my formative years.

Secondly, heartfelt thanks go to my loving husband, Erol, and my equally loving son, Kemal, for their encouragement and support.

I also wish to thank my friends, relatives, and colleagues, who have patiently listened to me discuss my challenges, my triumphs, and my disappointments.

I would be remiss if I did not also acknowledge the many wonderful teachers I have had throughout the years - in high school, at Pomona College, at UCLA, and at USC. They instilled in me a love of learning, of analysis, of critical thinking, and of the collective knowledge to which we all contribute.

About the Author

Erika Nomland Cilengir has always felt most at home in the land between art and science. Although an English major in college, she balanced her English classes with plenty of math and science classes. A career in technology gave her the best of both worlds. Cilengir has been the managing editor of the popular tea blog, TChing.com, and has written for *Forecast Journal*. Most recently, her poem, "When I Belong," was published in the anthology, *The Citadel 2022*. When Cilengir isn't writing, she is active in Toastmasters, walks and runs the streets of LA, leads a communication workshop for previously unhoused women, and enjoys time with her math tutor husband, street photographer son, and sweet pup. **Connect with Erika:**

www.tea4good.org **FB**: @ErikaCilengir **IG**: @erika.cilengir